MY HUNDRED-YEAR
MISSIONARY ADVENTURE

He taught hundreds of indigenous missionaries in the Philippines, reached an unreached tribe on Panay Island, announced the gospel to thousands of Filipinos through tent evangelism, strengthened a naval chapel in Puerto Rico, rescued a failing church in Hawaii, encouraged missionaries in Thailand, and built a Bible seminary in Leyte. Bill Hopper's legacy continues to expand while this centenarian continues to serve his Lord.

MY HUNDRED-YEAR
Missionary
Adventure

He reached the unreached Ati tribe & trained
nationals globally for missionary service

WILLIAM HOPPER
with JOHN LINDNER

ANM
publishers

MY HUNDRED-YEAR
Missionary Adventure

© 2019 by William Hopper, John Lindner
and Advancing Native Missions

ISBN: 978-1-946174-13-0 PAPERBACK

PUBLISHED BY:

Advancing Native Missions
P.O. Box 5303 • Charlottesville, VA 22905
www.AdvancingNativeMissions.com

GRAPHIC DESIGN BY: Christopher & Heather Kirk, GraphicsForSuccess.com, with cover contribution by Nathan Bowen

---

PHOTOS: Cover photo shows Bill and Naomi Hopper with Basalisa, daughter of Chief Severo, first Ati convert and pastor, in 2003. Photos in Chapter 9 are by John Lindner, while he served with Christian Aid Mission; photos used by permission. All other photos are from Bill Hopper's collection.

William Hopper taught hundreds of indigenous missionaries in the Philippines, reached an unreached tribe on Panay Island, announced the gospel to thousands of Filipinos through tent evangelism, strengthened a naval chapel in Puerto Rico, rescued a failing church in Hawaii, encouraged missionaries in Thailand, and built a Bible seminary in Leyte. Bill Hopper's legacy continues to expand while this centenarian continues to serve his Lord.

Dedication

I dedicate this book to my wife, Naomi, who for more than half of my life has been my companion, help-meet, and encourager through all the up-times and down-times that our Lord has carried us through.

William Hopper served in the navy in WW II, graduated from Moody Bible Institute in 1948 and was sent out by Association of Baptists for World Evangelism as a missionary to the Philippines. There he became president of Doane Bible Institute, carried on tent evangelism, and was instrumental in reaching the unreached Ati tribe. He later also served under United Faith Mission as an effective evangelist and church planter. He continues to encourage believers in the Philippines.

Contents

Preface

For many years my friends and family have urged me to "write a book" and publish the stories I was telling them. I wrote a few stories and filed them away but did not know how to publish them. Recently a representative of Advancing Native Missions" (ANM) was assigned to visit me and interview me to write the story of my one-hundred years of life. This book is the result of many hours spent with writer John Lindner. We thank the mission and John for making it possible for you to read about the work of God in one very long life.

During the long life that the Lord has given me, I have had many experiences. They vary in length and importance. For instance, the first twenty-five years of my life were quite ordinary. I spent my first 18 years with my parents and one brother. We spent only a few years in any location. This resulted in my having no boyhood friends to keep in touch with. Our parents were clean, moral people. My father was a preacher, but only espoused the social gospel of his denomination. As a result, people regarded me as "a good little preacher's son." But I did not hear the gospel.

After graduation from high school, I went away to college, never to return to live with my parents. I enjoyed the freedom from parental control and sampled things in the world that attracted me. I avoided attending church. I had no religious life. I quit college to marry at age 19. I found it difficult to enter the workforce and support a family.

As shared in this book, my wife Dorothy and I lived a lifestyle of a typical young couple of that era. We had two daughters, advanced in the field of merchandising, and avoided anything spiritual. We found ourselves assigned to a position of work that took us to the town of Sturgis, Michigan. This is where our life was changed completely, as you will see. Dorothy and I spent sixteen years together on the mission field. We had two more children. Then she was diagnosed with breast cancer which took her to heaven at age 48.

The following year Naomi Hucal became my wife, and we have served the Lord together for fifty-two years. God has taken us to Puerto Rico, Hawaii, Thailand and then back to the Philippines, where we currently serve. The

Lord graciously gave us another son and daughter. This book shares some of our many adventures.

When God takes over a life, the entire picture is changed, as you will see. It is my prayer that this account of my one hundred years of experience will encourage and challenge the reader and glorify the Lord Jesus Christ, who has been our guide, protector and master for the past seventy-five years.

I want to thank my wife, Naomi, for her contributions to my memory, our daughter-in-law, Karyn, for her experienced aid in proofreading and helping to get the photos to our writer-editor, John Lindner, for his skill in putting all this together, and to all of those who contributed to the great adventure this book tells.

To God be the glory!

A Word from the Author

I was on a fact-finding mission to the Philippines for Christian Aid Mission in 1995. In my island hopping, I stopped at Leyte Baptist Evangelistic Institute (fast becoming Leyte Baptist Seminary) in Maasin on Leyte Island to visit David Epilepcia, with whom we were corresponding.

That was when and where I met William and Naomi Hopper. The energy and enthusiasm of the Hoppers and the entire team effort of founding a school to train gospel preachers and workers thrilled me. At that time, the school was meeting in the Maasin Baptist Church.

I got Bill Hopper's newsletters for a number of years, and then communication fell off. I was pleasantly surprised if not shocked when, in January 2019, Bo Barredo, co-founder of Advancing Native Missions, asked me if I would stop and spend a week in Hawaii on my way to India and write a book on the life of Bill Hopper. I was excited to meet the man who was still going strong at 100, and was even more thrilled when I learned of his adventurous life.

I visited Honolulu February 8-16, 2019, and in those eight days Bill dictated to me his life story. I had it completely in writing by the time I left Honolulu for India. I am glad I could be an amanuensis for a beloved missionary who can barely see because of advanced macular degeneration. Though I wrote the story, I put it in the first person, because, after all, that is the way he told it to me.

Foreword
BY PETE WONG

God must have a great sense of humor in moving Pastor Bill Hopper to ask me to write this Foreword. Of his tens of hundreds of more able, nobler, closer friends and kin, for reasons unbeknownst to me, he asked me to do it.

Being an alumnus of Doane Baptist Bible Institute where Pastor Bill was once School President in the late 1940s, his name was very familiar with almost everyone associated with Doane—not just there in the entire island of Panay, but throughout Western Visayas of the Philippine archipelago among Fundamental Baptist churches. It was not until the early 1990's that my wife Melody and I met him in person for the first time in Thailand. We were missionaries sent there at that time by our home church, the Manila Baptist Church, and another

100 churches affiliated with the Association of Fundamental Baptist Churches in the Philippines (AFBCP). We served there in that Buddhist country 1986-1996 as cross-cultural church planters and Bible-school faculty with the Philippine Association of Baptists for World Evangelism (PABWE).

We had just returned from our first missionary furlough when Pastor Bill and Auntie Naomi Hopper left his thriving pastoral ministry in Honolulu, Hawaii to labor among international English-speaking expatriates, pastoring a fledgling new and small congregation, the Fellowship Baptist Church, in Bangkok, the nation's capital. What astounded me was--and still does today—is that he did this in his early 70's!

It was an honor and a privilege to have worked with the Hoppers, assisting them in their Thailand ministry. For two years, Melody and I would join them at their services on Sunday evenings, commuting across town from our mission station in the Ratburana district to where they were in the Bangkhen district. He would have us lead the music and the singing while he did the preaching and teaching. Auntie Naomi meanwhile would direct the potluck fellowship meal afterward, serving her to-die-for home-cooked Filipino dishes along with her world-famous cinnamon rolls and other mouth-watering desserts she baked herself.

Pastor Hopper's pulpit ministry at Fellowship Baptist Church displayed the Holy Spirit's gifts of anointed exhortation and forth-telling, edifying the body of Christ and glorifying his Savior. Besides his erudite preaching and teaching, Melody and I witnessed his passion for the lost, reaching out even to his alcoholic expat neighbors and friends he jokingly called his "beer-drinking buddies," though he, himself, is a teetotaler. His practice was more Christ-like than that of any of us (Luke 15:1ff).

On top of all this, we cherished the special time we had together with this august couple when every week they would host our overnight stay at their modest yet comfortable house in the next district north of Bangkhen. Having no ride of our own, and when returning to our mission station at night meant spending two hours of commuting across town if public transportation were available, Melody and I thankfully received the Hoppers' selfless hospitality and great company on Sunday nights. It was awesome fellowship that lasted till late Monday morning, Mondays being what we in the ministry call the missionary's Sabbath.

It was a wonderful symbiosis as well. The Hoppers being first-term Thailand missionaries needed help adjusting to their new mission field from us second-termers. Just communicating in the Thai vernacular was already a challenge. In the early 1990's it was especially difficult to get around Metropolitan Bangkok without a working knowledge of conversational Thai.

Their ministry's focus on English-speaking expats sometimes involved visiting some of them in jail. The four of us would join our seasoned fellow missionaries to go into these prisons and minister to the expat inmates. And although this focus didn't require it, Bill and Naomi still tried to learn to speak Thai. At the end of their time of ministry in Thailand, Acharn (anglicized Thai word อาจารย์ for Pastor) Hopper put it in his own inimitable, self-effacing way, "Two years ago, I prayed God would give me the gift of the Thai tongue. So far, I'm just tongue-tied."

Over two decades later in 2015, as God would have it, our paths crossed again, this time in the Philippines. As Southeast Asia Regional Director and Administrator of Advancing Native Missions, us Wongs were visiting our ministry partners in the island of Leyte and heard that Acharn Bill, at age 97, and Auntie Naomi were still busy serving the Lord, teaching future pastors, evangelists and church planters at the Leyte Bible Seminary in Maasin. So, we hopped, skipped and jumped over to see them and fellowship with them once more.

In November 2018, Melody and I found ourselves as two of the more than 200 guests who gathered together at Honolulu Bible Church in Honolulu, Hawaii, celebrating Acharn Bill Hopper's 100th birthday!

God took great pleasure in knitting together our hearts with those of the Hoppers, not just as friends and brethren in the faith, but also as fellow laborers in our heavenly Father's harvest fields. We eventually find out that while he was Doane president (late 1940's and early 1950's) in the Philippines, Acharn Bill reached out to the Ati tribe, the aboriginal Filipinos, in the town of Nagpana in Iloilo province. The Lord of the Harvest used Acharn Hopper as the first American missionary to reach the Ati for Christ.

Through his Gospel preaching, the first Ati who came to faith in Christ was a tribal chieftain named Severo Elosendo who later became the first pastor of the Ati church. Little did we know that one of Advancing Native Missions' current Southeast Asia ministry partners, Rogelio Elosendo, was the nephew of and successor to his late Uncle Severo's ministry leadership among the Ati.

Half-jesting yet most seriously speaking, when I grow up, I want to be like the Reverend Doctor William Dale Hopper. May this biography be an inspiration to its readers and a faithful witness and testimony to what God can do through a man entirely devoted to love his God with all his heart, with all his soul, and with all his mind, and to love his neighbor as himself. May he receive the sweetest words anyone can hear from his Savior when he finally meets Him face to face, "Well done, thou good and faithful servant. Enter now into the joy of thy Lord."

Pedro "Pete" Galvez Wong, Jr.
Missions Advocate
Advancing Native Missions

CHAPTER 1

Bill Hopper—
Birth to Rebirth

I was born in Minear, Illinois, a sleepy town near Peoria, on November 13, 1918, two days after the armistice of WW I. My second-generation British mother, Barbara, was only 18; my Holland-Dutch father, Lewis Dee, was a circuit-riding Methodist preacher.

The very next year, Dad was assigned to Park City, Utah, a mining town that later became famous for its skiing. He was there only one year when his father died, and he moved back to Illinois to take care of his mother. Dad became a traveling salesman in the early 20s, to acquire funds to further his education at McKendree College in

Illinois. He then returned to the circuit rider ministry in the hills of southern Illinois.

The family settled in Crab Orchard, Illinois. The place had no electricity, and the family used a wood cooking stove and fireplace. Dad Hopper rode a horse to his circuit of two churches—one in Crab Orchard, and the other

Billy Hopper as a young boy

out in the boonies. The dirt roads were almost impassable in the rainy season.

Crab Orchard is no longer there. They dammed up Crab Orchard Creek in the early 30s, and the place is now a 9,000+ acre Crab Orchard Lake.

We moved next to Mt. Vernon, Illinois; then to Carbondale in 1923. That was where I began Kindergarten. We stayed there for only two years.

Next, we went to a coal-mining town called Royalton. But soon Dad was transferred to Mt. Auburn. Dad had the distinction of putting up a new church building while there.

When I was in 3rd grade, we moved to Iileopolis, Illinois, where we stayed for three years. When I got my first bicycle for Christmas, I was so excited I went outside and shoveled a path through four inches of snow so I could try it out immediately.

I also had a friend in school that wore eyeglasses. I thought his glasses were neat, and I wanted a pair too, though I didn't need them. But I wanted them so bad I walked past my house on the way home and told Mom, "My eyes are so bad I couldn't see the house!" She didn't buy it.

When I was ten years old, I began delivering the morning newspaper from Decatur and the evening paper from Springfield to our town's 400 residents. I also sold all the Crowell magazines including *Ladies Home Journal, Women's Home Companion, The Saturday Evening Post, Colliers,* and others. I had a monopoly of Crowell magazines in the area. People even called me "the little Jew," because I was always selling something.

After three years in Iileopolis, Dad was transferred to Peoria and became a fundraiser for the Methodist hospital there. I graduated from the 8th grade in Peoria. The next year I had hardly started high school, when Dad was transferred to Pontiac, Illinois, to pastor a church near there. We barely scraped by for the next two years.

But it was 1932, the country was in the depths of the Great Depression, and the church could not pay the $50 per month it had promised. So, Mother made bread and sold it door-to-door. Farmers would invite Dad out when they butchered and give him some meat.

In the middle of my junior year, the bishop assigned Dad to Assumption. While there I became very active in Boy Scouts and even became a counselor in a Boy Scout camp on Lake Decatur. There was supposed to be a World Jamboree in Washington D.C. that year, and the Boy Scout group from our area had raised enough funds to attend. We were rarin' to go when suddenly the Jamboree was canceled because of the polio epidemic in 1934. Since we already had the money, we instead went to Detroit, Niagara Falls, New York City, and Washington D.C. by train. We visited the shredded wheat factory in Niagara Falls and were fed shredded wheat with milk and sliced bananas.

I was half-way through my senior year of high school when the district transferred Dad to Macon, Illinois, near Decatur. So that's where I graduated. There were 36 graduates in our class of 1936.

Because my father was a Methodist preacher, I got a half-tuition scholarship the next year to Illinois Wesleyan in Bloomington, a Methodist school. I had learned to swim in the Boy Scouts and swam on the swimming team. And since the school made knowing how to swim a requirement for graduation, I earned some money as a college swimming instructor. I majored in math and engineering.

During my second year, I met Dorothy McCormick. Neither of us was a Christian at that time. Though Dad was a minister, he was not a gospel preacher. He majored in the social gospel popular at the time and admired by the likes of Harry Emerson Fosdick, who said he didn't believe in the Virgin birth and didn't know any educated person who did. Dad preached we should live according to the Golden Rule and the Sermon on the Mount. He always ended his prayer, with "...and in heaven, at last, save us." He knew no assurance of salvation, and I was not saved.

Dorothy and I even lied about our age to get a marriage license. We were only 19, but you had to be 21 to get a marriage license, without parental consent, so I told them we were 21. In 1938 birth records were not required—many had none—and so the marriage was permitted.

I quit college and went to work for a shoe company—Miller Jones Shoes (originated in Ohio). When I turned 21, the company made me manager of the shoe store in DeKalb, Illinois. My salary was $25 a week.

I soon realized I had gone as far as I could in that company, so I quit and got a job with Montgomery Ward in Ottowa, Illinois. They put me in their manager training program, and every time they promoted me, they assigned me to a different store. They sent me to Benton Harbor, Michigan. Dorothy and I were still unsaved and by then had two daughters.

In 1942, they transferred me to Sturgis, Michigan. I still was not going to church, but while there, I decided to start going to church—a Methodist Church. All the pastor preached about was needing more money, so we decided to try the Presbyterian Church. On our first visit, the pastor said to me, "We need a leader for our young people; would you be willing to help us?" He didn't know anything about me. That turned us off.

I was assistant manager in Sturgis. I had to get the merchandise out on the floor and supervise the part-time workers. Ira Mead was a full-time printer who worked part-time on Thursday nights and Saturdays. He began witnessing to me and kept inviting me to the gospel hall. He was Plymouth Brethren and knew that the people, not the building, was the church. I just thought "gospel hall" sounded like "holy rollers."

It was summer time. The church was conducting Vacation Bible School. "Would you like to send your daughter?" he asked me. "OK," I agreed, as I thought, I get a baby sitter for a couple of weeks. Earl Froh, whose legs were crippled from polio, picked her up in his car and took her to VBS.

We were surprised at things Barbara learned there. We appreciated it so much we decided to give them some money to help with VBS. Dorothy offered Earl $5. He told her, "Thank you, but we don't accept money from the unsaved."

We were disgusted, but got convicted, and decided to

go to the "Gospel Hall" and see what those weird people were like who wouldn't take our money. They didn't allow outsiders to their "Breaking of Bread" service but welcomed us to their preaching service that followed.

Peter Pell from Grand Rapids was preaching that night. For the first time, we heard that we were sinners and needed to be saved. We also met a family who was our neighbors. Shirley Griffeth and his wife had two married daughters living with them while their husbands were serving in the war. They were our age; they visited us and loved our children.

They never sat down and urged us to accept Christ, but they were praying and would answer any questions. Finally, the father gave me a booklet, "Safety, Certainty and Enjoyment" by George Cutting. It was financed and published by Queen Mary of England and is still available today. I read it and accepted Christ after reading it. I gave it to Dorothy without comment. A couple of weeks later, I asked her, "Did you read the booklet?"

"Yes, and I accepted Christ on October 9, 1943."

One month later, the company transferred me to Aurora, Illinois. I went ahead of the family to find a place to live. It was November, and on Thanksgiving Day I wanted to be with somebody who knew the Lord. I stumbled upon a group of believers meeting in the YMCA. The second time I attended they asked me to sing, and I sang for them, "No One Ever Cared for Me Like Jesus."

I moved my family down soon after that and introduced them to the Baptist Church belonging to the General Association of Regular Baptists (GARB).

I knew that the next promotion with Montgomery Ward would be to manage my own store. But I became convicted that I should be serving the Lord. I enjoyed my work with the store, but I lost all interest in upward mobility. One day I abruptly said to Dorothy, "I think we should go to Bible school. After the Christmas rush is over, I'm going to resign from Montgomery Ward, and we'll go to Bible School." She gladly affirmed my decision.

CHAPTER 2

World War II Interlude

I wasn't mature enough to ask the Lord for guidance. In mid-December I received a letter from the government stating my draft status was 1-A, meaning I would be drafted. I thought, *If I'm going to be drafted, I'd rather enlist in the Navy than dig foxholes with the Army.*

So, I went to the Navy recruiter. He said, "We've got a school in Chicago you might be able to get into. If you can pass the test, we'll put you in electronic school for 11 months." I went, took the test, and even though I didn't think I did very well, I passed it. In two weeks, I received noticed to report to Great Lakes Naval Station. Eager to get men in school, they sent me out immediately.

I had one month of school in Chicago, followed by three months in Gulf Port, Mississippi. There I met a Christian officer and told him I was going to be a missionary. He said, "How do you know? Pray about it. Talk to the Lord and see what He says." I wrote Dorothy and told her that. We covenanted to pray and ask the Lord what He wanted us to do after the war.

I had not been baptized. Baptism doesn't save; why should I be baptized? While in Gulf Port, I found a church that was closed due to lack of a pastor. So about six of us Navy guys decided to open the church, and one of us preached every Sunday. The issue of baptism came up, so we asked a retired pastor if he would baptize all of us.

After three months' training, I was sent back to Chicago to finish school on Navy Pier. At that time, it was just an old pier sticking out into Lake Michigan. In the school, we were loaded down with electronics. We studied a new subject each week. If we passed that test, we went on to the next test. If we failed, we repeated the week. Three repeats and we were out. Only 25% of us survived. The whole course took eleven months.

While I was taking these courses, I went to a Christian Business Men's service center. It offered a lounge, food, and Bible studies. I met one man who was involved with the Navigators. He introduced me to their topical Bible study and memorization program, which helped me grow in the Lord. They sent out gospel teams of servicemen to various churches. The people were thrilled to hear men in uniform give

Bill the Sailor

their testimonies. I made lots of contacts with churches in the Chicago area, which helped me greatly later on.

I graduated from the class as a 3rd class petty officer. I never went any higher.

They sent me to Treasure Island in San Francisco Bay for further assignment (FFA). I had heard that servicemen could get me a job on the railroad. I got a job washing dishes, and that enabled me to bring Dorothy and our two daughters out to be with me. The railroad provided food, lodging, transportation and $25 cash. But I worked there only two days, just enough time to get from Chicago to San Francisco.

When Dorothy and the girls arrived, they stayed with friends from the Navigators in San Francisco. But they

11

could not visit me, and I could not go to them. We could only talk to each other on the telephone.

We had to fill out a questionnaire. One of the questions was, "What would you like to be assigned to?"

"An island," I wrote down, "not a ship."

They assigned me and 13 others to the amphibious force (landing craft) and sent us to Pearl Harbor to learn how to operate Army Navy equipment. From there, they put me on an LST (Landing Ship Tank, meaning it could carry and offload tanks) and sent all 14 of us to Guam FFA. That's where the big bombers bombing Japan were stationed. The trip took us 21 days.

It was then 1945. The naval station was not complete; there was no chapel and no officers' mess. Neither were there any regular worship services. But two things happened: one by one the other 13 men were sent out on different vessels, and I was the only one left. Then about six weeks later I found a Bible study conducted by Lieutenant Vanderbreggen. I had to sneak off the base to attend his Bible study because he was a Marine.

One night I was doing my own Bible reading, and I heard someone singing a hymn. I followed the sound, and down in one corner of the base was a temporary shack and a few men—all black. From outside I looked in, and out of the darkness a booming voice said, "Come on in, brother." That began a practice of fellowshipping with them.

One day I went to the office and asked why I was still here. They found my orders in a file cabinet. The orders assigned me to LCI 789 (landing craft infantry); it could carry 250 men from troop-carrier ships to shore. They put me on a repair ship headed to Ulithi in the South Pacific and eventually dropped me off there. I was assigned a bunk but given no orders. There was no LCI. I waited a week.

They couldn't find the LCI to which I was assigned. So, they put me on a tanker and sent me to the Philippines. We landed at Guiuan on Eastern Samar Island. They were building a naval and air station there in preparation for an attack on Japan. They had already made a runway for the big bombers. But there were no comfort facilities. We had to bathe in the ocean and rinse off with a bucket of fresh water.

Two weeks later they put me on another ship and sent me to the Leyte Gulf. They stationed me on a floating barracks, a tethered barge. They still could not find LCI 789. Leyte Gulf was filled with hundreds of ships of all sizes, preparing to invade Japan.

One day I was up on the deck and saw LCI 789 pass by. I watched it, and it ended up at a place across the bay. I told those in charge, and they put me on a personnel carrier and got me there. There was nobody around. Someone took me to the officer in charge. He told me LCI

789 had just arrived from Borneo. It had been the flagship control center for 13 LSMs. The LSMs (landing ship medium) could carry two trucks or one tank. The officer said, "We'll put you on one of the LSMs later." It never happened. LCI 789 had bunks for staff below deck.

They showed movies every night; I used the time for Bible study and prayer. The guys saw me studying the Bible and called me "preacher." One day one of them said, "Hey, preacher, why don't you have church for us?"

I figured they were testing me, so I answered, "If you get permission, I'll do it."

He got permission. The chief officer of the LCI said, "We've got boxes of Bibles and hymnals that have never been opened. You can use them."

We had a Jewish yeoman (secretary) who had a mimeograph and volunteered to print a bulletin with the order of service. From the time we started until the war ended everybody who was not on duty was there. But when the war ended, attendance declined. No one made a decision for Christ during those days.

It was July 1945, and the attack on Japan seemed to be drawing closer. There were going to be two task forces: one to go to the north first to attract the kamikazes. The second would go to the south as part of the Pincer movement. We didn't know this until after the war. McArthur had almost finished in liberating the Philippines.

Dorothy and I had been praying and corresponding by letter what the Lord would have us do after the war. While there in Leyte Gulf—I never got on shore, never met a Filipino—the Lord impressed on me, *this is where I want you to be a missionary.*

My wife was back in Illinois, and pregnant. "Where I am now is where I believe God wants us to be missionaries," I wrote her. Before she received that letter, she wrote, "I am attending a missionary conference, and believe God wants me to be a missionary, but how can I go forward with two young girls and pregnant, without you? I need to wait for you."

Those two letters crossed in the mail. God was leading us both to a decision for missions, even though we were 10,000 miles apart.

In August the atomic bombs were dropped. The invasion was canceled, Japan surrendered, and the war ended. LCI 789 was assigned to a flotilla carrying occupation troops to Korea. We headed out in September and sailed into a typhoon; the waves were so big, we couldn't see the rest of the flotilla; we had to navigate by radar.

Our destination was Incheon. Seoul then was just a town of shacks, nothing to be desired. Now it is a beautiful city. Our assignment was to be the traffic directors. The average tide at Incheon is 17 feet. In order to use the port, they had built locks and used small cargo carriers to bring goods in from the ships to the docks. When it was low tide, the barges were out unloading the ships, and when it was high tide, they would come in through the locks to the docks. The locks would then be closed to maintain water level and let the barges unload. Our job was to tell each barge when to go in and where to go.

The government began discharging troops on a points system. If you had three children, you automatically had enough points to be discharged. My son was born on October 31. We were on a small vessel and didn't have big brass to deal with. The officer in charge said, "As soon as you have proof of the birth of your third child, you can go."

We received the affidavit from the doctor on my birthday, November 13, 1945. Because of our job, we knew where each ship was located and where they were going. A troop carrier loaded with army guys was leaving for home the next day. It had a few bunks available for "passengers" (Navy), and I was on my way home the very next day.

We landed in Portland. I was put in a station for transportation to Great Lakes Naval Station for discharge. While in Portland, I found a Christian servicemen's center and got acquainted with some Christian men. One evening two young sailors came in. I sat with them and began witnessing to them. Both of them received the Lord as their Savior.

Finally, I was put on a train and sent to Great Lakes. There I was given my discharge papers and sent home to Ottowa, Illinois. I opened the door and walked straight to the crib to see my son. "You didn't even kiss me," Dorothy said. "You walked right past me to see your son." We made up, and all was well.

CHAPTER 3

Getting to the Field

Home in Ottawa, Illinois, I made inquiries where to live in Chicago so we could go to Moody Bible Institute. Our friends told us, "If you had three dogs, no problem, but three kids—no way." Someone told me of a Christian guy who had just bought a three-story apartment house, with two apartments in the basement. He said he would give us one of the basement apartments free if we would be managers of the building. In the middle of the room was a steam pipe at head level—I had to duck to get past it—and only two windows across the front end where you could see people walking by from their knees down.

My mother was disgusted. "You're bringing your family up here to live in this cave?"

We moved in in January 1946. Every week we had to clean three apartments, take out the trash, and make sure all the tenants had adequate heat. I had to shovel snow when needed.

I got a job in the shipping room at Sears at nights and enrolled part-time at Moody. When our children started kindergarten, they rode the streetcar to school. We did that for one school year.

We heard they were having a missionary conference at Belden Avenue Baptist Church. Missionaries to the Philippines were speaking, so we went to see what we could find out. That was our first contact with the Association of Baptists for World Evangelism. Harold Commons, president of ABWE, was there, and ABWE missionary Ruth Woodworth also spoke. She had been interred by the Japanese for four years during the war.

We introduced ourselves to her after the service and told her we were interested in going to the Philippines. My wife was wearing a fur coat. Ruth looked at us and said, "Well, dear people, it's not romantic on the mission field." Dorothy took off her gloves showing her reddened hands and said, "Mrs. Woodworth, it's not romantic scrubbing floors to put your husband through Bible school, either." Mrs. Woodworth didn't say anything more.

We never contacted another mission. The Lord showed us that was where He wanted us.

The next school year, I wanted to enroll full time. When I did, I found out that if I had tried to enter when I received my 1A draft letter, I could not have done so. They had a rule that you had to be saved one full year before you enrolled. They wanted people with some spiritual growth and maturity behind them. Once again, we saw the providence of God.

I started full-time classes, commuting by elevated train. One of my professors was Dr. McCarrel from Cicero Bible Church in Cicero, Illinois, a suburb of Chicago. He was one of the founders of the IFCA. In talking with him, I learned that Cicero Bible Church had small daughter churches throughout the area. I applied to pastor one of the branches called Douglas Park Bible Mission on Chicago's Southside. It was in a neighborhood of Bohemian Catholics. In the same block as the mission were four taverns. The mission met in the store building and had a small one-bedroom apartment behind it. We had a free apartment again, and $10 per-week salary. We were prospering!

This little apartment was heated with a gas space heater. There was a toilet but no bathtub or shower. We had to bathe in a tub in the kitchen. But it was God's provision. The storefront could accommodate 25 people for meetings.

One elderly lady, a member of the mission, had been

converted in the evangelistic meetings of D.L. Moody and consequently thought she owned the place. The first Sunday I preached, I made the announcements, and then asked, "Are there any other announcements?" She stood up and said, "Yes, I have a special number." She read a poem and sang a song, and then sat down.

We needed more income. A business district the next block down had a shoe store. I talked to the owner, Morris. I explained my background in the shoe business and asked him if I could have a job there. He said, "I'd be glad to have you come in on Thursdays and Saturdays." Perfect.

I never lied about the size of a shoe. If a woman wearing a size 8 thought she wore size 6 and asked for it, I wouldn't give her a size 8 and tell her I was giving her a size 6. Morris appreciated my honesty and said, "Just let me take those customers."

A fellow student from the area had a car. I got to ride with him instead of taking the El. Also riding with us was John Peterson, who later became famous for his hymns.

I enrolled in the missionary-pastor course. Dorothy had her hands full with the children but was able to take a few classes from time to time. The school accepted some of my previous college credits, and I stayed on through the summer completing three semesters per year. So, I was able to complete the four-year course in two-and-a-half years and graduated in August 1948.

Pastors of various churches in Chicago gave me contacts with ABWE, and I was accepted as a missionary before I graduated. My home church in Ottawa ordained me before I graduated from Bible school. By the time I graduated, I was ready to do deputation.

The Hopper family in 1948

Then Morris said, "Hopper, you've been so good to me. Would you manage my store full time for one month so I could take a vacation?"

I said, "You have two men working here full time. Can't you use one of them?"

He said, "I can't trust them, but I can trust you."

So I managed the shoe store during September 1948.

My home church had pledged support; some others had pledged support. I contacted some of the churches I had testified in while I was at Great Lakes. Three months later, I had my full support. A lot of churches had had their missions program disrupted because of the war and were ripe for someone to support. But support then was far less then than it is now. My goal was just $900 per month. I was ready to be sent out by ABWE.

ABWE was born in the Philippines when the American Baptist Foreign Missionary Society had forbidden Dr. Raphael Thomas to do evangelism outside his medical work.

Some co-workers complained that Dr. Thomas spent too much time doing evangelistic work and not enough time in the hospital. At that time the divide between liberals and fundamentalists was reaching its peak. When his mission board told him in 1927 to stick to medicine and leave the preaching to theologically trained missionaries, he resigned, returned to the U.S., and shared his vision with Mrs. Marguerite Doane and several others in Philadelphia.

Mrs. Doane's father had been a highly successful industrialist millionaire as well as a famed hymnwriter who had put 1,500 of Fanny Crosby's poems to music. He passed away in 1915, and Marguerite inherited his fortune. She and two other ladies met in Philadelphia in 1927 to discuss the mission situation. As a result, they formed the Association of Baptists for Evangelism in the Orient (ABEO) with Lucy Peabody as its first president. When the organization sent its first missionary to Peru in

1939, it changed its name to the Association of Baptists for World Evangelism.

I went to Philadelphia, met Mrs. Doane, and had my credentials reviewed by the board. ABWE booked passage for us on the British cargo vessel S. S. Swansea. It left from New York Harbor and could carry 12 passengers. Accommodations were excellent. Dorothy and I had a stateroom and each child—David 4, Dee Ann 8, Barbara 11—had their own room. The crew even made a hatch into a small pool about 10 x 10 for the kids. The officers were all British. Part of the crew were Muslims, who worked below deck, and the other part Hindus, who worked above deck.

We stopped in many ports to load and unload, went through the Panama Canal, up the West Coast to San Diego and San Francisco, and from there straight across the Pacific to Manila. Total time was 51 days. We traveled that way two different times before there was air travel. Subsequent generations of missionaries referred to us who traveled to the mission field aboard cargo ships as "the boat people."

The ABWE missionaries met us in Manila, which was still in shambles from the war; many sunken vessels cluttered Manila Bay. We stayed there a week and then I was assigned to teach in Doane Evangelistic Institute in Iloilo City, the provincial capital city of Panay. That

Doane Baptist Evangelistic Institute of that era

was ABWE's first Bible school, established in 1923, though its service had been interrupted by the war from 1941 to 1945. When we arrived in February 1949, it had only 14 students.

Language foibles

"You don't need to learn the language," a veteran missionary told me. "Almost everyone here speaks English. For those who don't, you can always get an interpreter." In most foreign countries, one must speak the language to communicate. In the Philippines, English is common, as it is the medium of education and is encouraged.

Even so, I was convinced that all missionaries should study the language of the people to whom God sends them. How can we convince them that we are sincerely concerned for their souls if we are not interested enough to learn their language? One Filipino said to me, "English speaks to my head, but Ilonggo speaks to my heart." So, I pursued to learn Ilonggo, the language of my region, one of 87 dialects spoken in the Philippines.

I inquired about study material for learning the language. "Sorry, none." My search did lead to the procurement of an out-of-print English-Ilonggo dictionary. This book was as big as the usual concordance and was prepared by a Roman Catholic priest many years before. It was a significant find and greatly aided my study.

Another discovery was a small book entitled How to Learn a Language, written by an American missionary to India. It contained a simple plan for the study of any language. With the assistance of a dear Filipina lady, I studied the helps in the book. I even wrote out a simple sermon to be used when the opportunity presented itself.

Bill Hopper, President of DBEI

The time came when I was invited to preach in a local church. With shaking knees, I proceeded to stumble through my prepared message. The laughing of the congregation from time to time led me to think I made a total mess of the language and simply amused the people with my errors. I said to the pastor after the service, "I guess I really messed up that attempt!"

"Oh no," he replied.

"Well, why did they laugh so much?"

"They were just expressing their pleasure that you would attempt to preach in their language."

Today, seventy years after my first arrival on the mission field, there are language schools in the Philippines where missionaries can study the major dialects and distinctive cultures of various people groups.

All of us missionaries have had humorous experiences in the process of using a newly-learned language. However, it is a mistake to allow these errors to make us ashamed to keep trying.

I remember one of my first "boo-boo's. I was talking to an elderly lady at church. She greeted me with the most common word, "Komusta?" I proudly replied, "Maayo ayo." I thought I told her "I am well." She just smiled politely. Her daughter saw that I was puzzled and informed me that I had told her I was beautiful!

One of our most fluent missionary friends also made mistakes. He went to the kitchen in his home where the lady helpers were eating their dinner. He intended to ask them if they were full. He should have used the word, "busug," but he inadvertently asked "Busung kamo?" which meant, "Are you pregnant?"

Two single missionaries were served sweet rice cooked with brown sugar and coconut milk called "bico." One of the ladies told the hostess, "Oh, bitok, I love bitok." Her compliment reflected her medical clinic background. She actually said that she loved intestinal parasites.

The joke was not always on the missionaries. One of our missionary men, who became fluent in Ilonggo, was riding in an outrigger canoe from one island to another. The men on the canoe, unaware that the Americano could understand their conversation, said in the dialect, "Let's throw the Americano overboard." The missionary laughed and said in Filipino, "Go ahead. I can swim!"

There is not room to tell all the amusing stories of mistakes made by language students. May the Lord con-

Doane Baptist Bible Institute today

tinue to help all those currently studying the languages necessary to minister to the millions of unreached people of the world.

CHAPTER 4

Reaching the Ati

While I was at Moody, I had tried to learn as much as I could about the Philippines. I saw a pamphlet, "The Ati of Panay," put out by the U.S. government. I read that, and the Lord kept it in my mind. I was amazed when the mission assigned me to Panay.

After I was settled in and was teaching, I asked, "Can anyone help me find the Ati?"

One student asked, "Why?"

"So, I can find out if they have ever heard the gospel," I answered.

"Why, sir, they don't even have a soul, do they?" he replied.

I learned that the locals considered them one level above the animals.

I finally found a Filipino pastor who knew an Ati half-breed named Augustine. His father was a mainland Filipino (often called a lowlander) while his mother was an Ati.

The lowlanders are Malayan. The Ati are Negroid. The Ati were the original inhabitants, long before the Malayans arrived.

The Ati are nomadic, hunters and gatherers. They have no education, no organized religion, no hygiene, and never intentionally take a bath. They wander through jungles, and hunt and live off the land. They are pacific; they don't fight; when confronted, they just retreat.

Augustine told the Ati chiefs that a tall white man was coming to visit them. There is a chief or head man in each clan. The clan we visited had only 200 people.

So we went to the Ati gathering place near Pitogo, in the foothills of the mountains, Augustine leading the way. Some boys carried Bill's accordion. The ladies brought flannelgraph materials. We came to a place where the Ati would care for sick people and those unable to travel. But there was nobody in sight.

We wondered what had happened. Then Severo, the chief, stepped out from behind a tree. He was wearing tattered shorts and a dirty T-shirt that looked like one had just wiped the car with it. Bill greeted him in English, which Augustine translated into Ilonggo, which the Ati also know, besides their own language. Augustine told Severo that Bill was acceptable.

Severo turned around and gave a shout, and about 20 Ati came out of the jungle. I played the accordion, taught them some choruses

Ati natives

in Ilonggo, and a student gave stories in flannelgraph. When we talked to the chief, he said that the lowlanders had told him that if the big white man comes, he will capture you and use your people for fuel in the sugar factories. That was why they had been hiding.

The issue that faced me was this: I was vastly interested in reaching these despised and unreached people with the gospel. At the same time, I was a full-time teacher at Doane Evangelistic Institute. I didn't want to go off on a tangent with the Ati at the expense of my teaching. So, we made arrangements to revisit them a month later.

We went back once a month for several months, and every time we spoke to about 15 to 25 Atis. When I finally gave the invitation, the chief immediately raised his hand. We talked and prayed with him. He was the only one.

The next time we gave an invitation, Severo stood up, held up his hand, and then turned around and commanded everybody, "Raise your hands!"

Severo was definitely saved. The others accepted Christ by obedience. We would follow them all up somehow.

Diet of the Ati

We all know that food varies in each foreign country. Ethnic food restaurants invite us to try delicacies of Japan, China, Mexico, Thailand, Europe, and others. But have you ever seen an advertisement for Ati food? I dare say you never will, so let me introduce you to some of the foods and eating habits of the indigenous people of the Philippines.

The primitive Ati have been nomadic hunters and root crop eaters for hundreds of years. Planting and harvesting were not part of their culture. When the hunting was depleted, they simply moved to another part of the jungle.

I had seen them hunting for birds, wild chickens, lizards, turtles, monkeys, and an occasional wild pig. They fished in the mountain streams for anything alive there, under the rocks or attached to sticks. However, it took many visits to gain their friendship and trust before the tribe invited me to eat with them.

My first such invitation came on a visit to a group of the little men who were camped on a hillside near the rice farms of the lowland. They were working in the rice harvest fields and would be paid with "humay" (rice in the husk). They would "mill" the humay by pounding it in a large wooden mortar with a wooden pestle. The hunters brought in six three-foot-long *haloes* pronounced (hah lo!). We call them monitor lizards in English. They are not scavengers but feed on birds and their eggs. The men built a fire and tossed the

The Ati love whole-roasted lizard.

lizards on the fire whole—no dressing or cleaning. While their reptile skin was sizzling and charring in the fire, a big pot of cleaned rice was cooking on another fire.

After a half an hour or so the lizards' scales were burned black as coal. It was not an appetizing sight or smell. They were removed from the coals and brought to the circle of men squatting around the pot of cooked rice. The charred skin was peeled away revealing the tender flesh. It had the appearance of chicken meat and tasted much the same.

As their spiritual mentor, I told them that we should pray and thank God for a successful hunt and the meal before us. As I asked them to bow their heads and close their eyes, Chief Severo leaned over to me and said quietly, "Sir, we cannot close our eyes while we pray, or the dogs might steal the food from us." I remembered that Jesus told us to "watch, and pray."

At other times birds and wild chickens were dressed and roasted on a spit. Most of the time the Ati had no rice, so they dug root crops or plucked the plentiful green plantains, which they also roasted in the fire. They all were dry and tasteless to me.

The Ati did not use salt. For that reason, many of them suffered from enlarged thyroid. I took a picture of an old lady who had a huge goiter. Later I made a copy to give her, but she refused to believe that she was the one in the photo. She had never seen herself in a mirror or picture.

Because of the nomadic lifestyle of the indigenous people, cooking utensils were minimal or nonexistent. Food to be cooked could be wrapped in banana leaves. There were always plenty of wild bananas to supply leaves even when they had no fruit. And there was no need for dishwashing as they used no dishes, and the dogs licked the banana leaves clean before they were left to dry out or rot.

Many plants in the jungle provide fruit or leaves that are edible. The Ati, from years of experience, know them all. Nests of wild bees provide an occasional sweet treat as well. The eggs of wild chickens or birds were delicacies when available.

When a pig was trapped and killed, the hunters hacked it into large pieces, roasted them in the fire, and then shared with everyone in the tribe—no fancy cleaning or butchering. On special occasions, the whole pig would be placed on a pole and roasted over an open fire.

The Negritos also ate monkeys and fruit bats. Fruit bats, known as "flying foxes," are about the size of a small cat. Their wings, like smaller house bats, consist of skin and are three to four feet wide. They would skin the bats, slice the meat into strips, and then dry it in the sun like jerky. They would eat the jerky when fresh meat was not available.

When I stayed with them overnight, they made for me a little shelter four feet long and a foot-and-a-half wide (Ati size) made of one-inch-wide sticks, raised about 18 inches from the ground, so they could put a smoking fire under it to keep the mosquitoes away. A slanting roof of palm leaves covered it. When I slept in it, I had to curl up like a cat, because it was far too short for me.

It was not difficult for me to share their food as I am not a picky eater. I was to learn much later just how much of an impression this made on my dear friends. Later, I learned that Severo, in his testimony for the Lord, would say, "I know that God loves the Ati because He sent that big Americano to find us. He ate our food and slept with us and told us about Jesus."

More recently, since many of the Ati now live on their reservation, the supply of lizards has been substantially depleted. When we went to the village during our annual visit in 2012, Severo's daughter, Basalisa, hired a hunter to go far away and find a lizard to cook especially for us. This time the reptile was dressed, cleaned, and cooked "adobo" style with a spicy recipe of vinegar and soy sauce. It didn't taste as good as that first charred lizard we ate out on the hillside!

When Severo was studying at the Bible Institute, he was introduced to many new recipes, both Filipino and American. One day one of the students took him down to a local restaurant for a special treat—ice cream. Never having eaten such a treat, Severo looked around and saw others putting generous portions of soy sauce on their rice. When the ice cream came, he grabbed the soy bottle and followed their example. Have you tried a soy sauce Sunday?

So much has changed in the lives of the Ati these past sixty years. This is true of their eating, too. Those who have been exposed to the lowland people are now more accustomed to eating Filipino recipes. But back in the mountains, things go on as they did a hundred years ago.

Ati clothing

Ati men wore G-strings; Ati women wore skirts made of bark, no tops. They took the bark of certain trees and pounded it until it became soft; then they tied the pieces together with vines.

As we ministered to them, we did not try to change their clothing; we just taught them the Word of God. But as they became Christians, they wanted to wear clothes. So, we brought boxes of used clothing and distributed it to them. Some items were strange to them. You should have seen the men trying to figure out what to do with a brassiere. We had to tell them these things were for the women.

One time, Severo asked if he could be the one to hand them out. He said, "I want to build a church, and I want to give clothes to those who are willing to help." This made it possible for them to build a bamboo and palm-leaf meeting place.

Building the chapel was quite a challenge because all they had ever constructed before were those little sleeping lean-tos.

We did not teach them anything about hygiene, but as they saw that Christians were clean, they wanted to be clean also. These changes reflected their new life in Christ. Jesus changed them; we didn't.

Ati becomes evangelist

I began praying for a student who would feel called as a missionary to the Ati. I took several students with me each time, but none of them felt called to the Ati. God answered the prayer in an astounding way.

Chief Severo came down to the school. He was reticent to talk with me directly, but he spoke with an elderly lady who was the school cook. "I would like to learn how to read the Bible," he said. She came and told me. Immediately the light clicked on. *This is our man. Ati reaching the Ati—the perfect solution.*

I arranged for him to come to the Bible school. I then spoke with the students. "I know how you feel about the Ati," I told them. "You look down on them, you tease them, and say they don't even have a soul. Now this man is coming here to study the Bible. And if any of you bullies him, you will be out the door."

So Severo came, and we sent food with him for his wife and child each weekend he returned home. We both were about 30, though the chief did not know his birthday (or year). So I assigned him my birthdate. I felt a kinship with him.

We assigned a faculty member to teach him how to read, another to do simple math, another how to tell time, another how to sing. The boys in the dorm took him in as a brother. He had a great sense of humor and was ready to learn.

Severo eagerly learned much in one full year.

He was taught in Ilonggo, studied Bible in Ilonggo, and learned to read Ilonggo. Boys taught him hygiene: how to take a bath, brush his teeth, wash his clothes. He had never worn a pair of shoes. His feet were spread out almost as rectangles from being barefoot all his years. But he wanted a pair of shoes like the other boys. The only thing they found that fit him were high-top tennis shoes.

Every weekend, accompanied by a student, he went home to be with his wife and daughter. And we gave him food to take back to his family since he wasn't there to provide for them. One weekend, the student returned, but Severo was not with him. Severo had told the student to return without him because he had laundry to do. Monday, Tuesday and Wednesday went by, and still no Severo. On Thursday he came dragging into the campus very disheveled, wearing a big dirty bandage on his right arm. We took him to the school nurse, and she cleaned the infected wound and bandaged it.

While she was doing that, he shared what had happened. He had lied about staying home to do his laundry; instead, he had returned to his old life of hunting. He took his hunting dog with him to look for a big lizard. He found one that hid in the crevice in the rocks. While trying to reach in to pull the lizard out, his dog mistook his arm for the lizard and bit him. The Ati witch doctor told him he was going to die. So he prayed and finally came back to school, a very penitent student. "Sir, I will never do this again," he promised. And he didn't.

It was amazing how fast he learned. He stayed with us for one full school year. Because he made such progress, the faculty decided to give him a special certificate. He marched with the graduation class of 1952. One of the students told him, "I have two white sharkskin suits; I'll let you have the old one." When they were ready to march, they learned Severo had mistakenly put the new suit on, and the student wore the old suit.

From then on Severo devoted himself to spreading the gospel among the Ati, and gathered the first church in 1954. Years later at a gathering of about 50 Ati pastors, one Ati pastor gave this testimony: "You planted one seed; this is the harvest," and he swept his hand over the audience. There are now 80 Ati pastors and congregations spread throughout Panay and Guimaras. Most of these were the first- and second-generation believers of Severo's efforts.

Nagpana Reservation

Over the mountain from Pitogo is a beautiful valley with a mountain stream and waterfall. The Ati often hunted there and concluded they would like to live in that valley. It was government land.

The Philippine Vice President Lopez was living in Iloilo. Severo and I approached him and asked if the government would donate that land to the Ati. Several years passed as we continued to pray about it. Finally, the government said if 25 families would move there and farm it, they would make it a reservation.

At the end of 10 years, Nagpana Reservation of about 1,000 acres was approved. The Nagpana Fundamental Baptist Church was founded there in 1954. Today more than 100 families live there. Lowlanders are forbidden to live there.

When it was first approved, it was a two-hour hike from the road to the valley. As the years passed, roads were constructed and there now is a paved road all the way to the reservation. It ends right in front of the new Ati church.

Bill and Severo bonded for life.

43

First Ati teacher

Basalisa, Severo's only child, was the first Ati to get an education. She spent one year with us while she attended high school. The government saw that she was studying and promised her that if she graduated from high school, they would give her a full scholarship to college. They also told her if she obtained a degree in education, they would construct a primary school (grades 1-3) in the reservation. She served as the head teacher of that school for more than 30 years. She is now retired and plagued with dementia.

The reservation is under the jurisdiction of the town of Barotac Viejo, three miles from the reservation's entrance. Severo became close friends of the mayor. When Severo died in January 2004, the mayor sent 12 town trucks to transport the people down to the cemetery. I conducted a funeral service at the reservation, and then Severo was buried in the town cemetery, where a Filipino pastor conducted the interment service. The town council presented Basalisa with a plaque of appreciation for her father's life and work. Ati believers dedicated a new church building in his memory on April 2, 2006.

We try to have one big event among the Ati each year. In 2018 we provided transportation funds for the Ati pastors to come to the event, food for the attendees, and a monetary gift for each of the pastors. About

60 pastors attended, and some brought other key church people with them. It is a great encouragement to these once-despised people.

Rogelio Elosendo, Severo's nephew, became heir to Servo's ministry, an Elisha to his Elijah. Severo asked Rogelio to carry on the work when he became unable to do so. Rogelio's story is covered in the Epilogue.

CHAPTER 5

"In-Tents" Evangelism

Before the war, Dr. Thomas, representing the Baptists, and Dr. Hubbard, representing the Presbyterians, made a comity agreement and divided the Philippines down the middle to avoid duplication and competition. The Baptists took the western side including the western side of Negros Island (Negros Occidental), and the Presbyterians took the eastern side (Negros Oriental) and the islands of Bohol, Leyte, Samar, and Cebu. Similar agreements were made for other parts of the Philippines. So ABWE was working in Negros Occidental and Panay.

Before the war, Paul and Kay Fredrichsen did church-planting work in Negros Occidental through tent evangelism. But they were interned four years during the war. They returned after the war, but their health was not good, and they left the field in 1950. That left nobody doing any evangelistic work in Negros. Yet Negros was the source of students for Doane Evangelistic Institute.

The school had four couples training students, but there was nobody in Negros Occidental evangelizing the people or planting churches for our students to lead. I felt I should leave my teaching position and go out there and evangelize. The school agreed. So, Dorothy and I and the children left Iloilo in 1953 to evangelize Negros Occidental.

We went first to Bacolod City, about a 2-hour ferry trip from Iloilo. The Fredrichsens had used a big tent that would seat 500. I had never done anything like that, but I had watched them.

I learned how to do black light chalk drawing and polished up on how to play the accordion. I had studied piano as a youth, so I understood the keyboard, but I had to learn the chord buttons. I also added puppets to the presentations. I would take with me one of the Doane graduates as a Filipino evangelist and two Bible women. The Bible women did child evangelism and visitation. I did puppet shows and chalk drawings and led songs with the accordion. The Filipino pastor would use filmstrips of the life of Christ to preach the sermon in Ilonggo.

A peek at an "in-tents" evangelistic meeting

The huge pieces of canvas offered quite a challenge to this rookie field missionary. How do you get those three pieces fastened together? Where do we get enough men to raise it on twenty-five-foot poles? What keeps it from falling after we get it up?

Many questions came to my mind as we prepared to begin our first tent campaign. Several Filipino men who had helped erect the tent for earlier missionaries rounded up a dozen laborers. We laid out the canvas on the vacant lot where it would stand and laced the centerpiece to the two ends with strong ropes. After stretching the side cords around the sides, we were ready to lift the forty-by-sixty-foot tent up on the long bamboo poles.

Using two scissor-shaped supports of bamboo, the men lifted and shoved until the two center poles were erect. There was no need to place the poles in holes since the weight of the tent would hold them in place. When the canvas was hanging, the men inserted the side poles into their rings. Ropes fastened to the ground with steel stakes kept the poles standing. Axles from scrapped jeeps made strong anchors.

What an amazing sight this monster became as it stood amidst the small bamboo-and-palm-leaf houses. We strung bright pennants around the edge of the tent and placed outdoor Christmas lights at the peak of the poles. It looked like a Mediterranean ship with lights. We added lights around the perimeter, completing the decoration of the plain tan canvas. Wide-eyed passersby often asked, "Is this a circus, sir?"

Inside, we erected a platform and hung fluorescent lights. Angle iron frames with wooden planks for a seat and a back provided seating for 500 adults. Many of the children squatted on the ground. A portable generator provided power for the lights and PA system. We tested every piece of equipment before the meetings so there would be no delays for repairs during the meeting.

The Filipinos feared persecution from the Roman Catholics, who for centuries had dominated the culture. When the house lights in the tent were on, people hesitated to enter the tent. So, we just lit the platform lights, and people filled the seats quickly. Perhaps they did not want to be seen entering this strange vessel. Night after night the benches were packed with 500 to 600 listeners.

I started the meeting with singing accompanied on the accordion. Filipinos love to sing, and they learned the songs quickly. We would hear the children singing the songs during the day as they played near the tent.

The Gospel Tent provided an intense exposure to the gospel.

After the song service, I presented the gospel through "Magic Chalk Drawings." The "magic" was the black light shining on the fluorescent chalk. I felt it was a great accomplishment when I was fluent enough in the dialect to preach and draw at the same time. After I completed a drawing, it was awarded as a prize in promotional contests. We still see these drawings gracing the walls of Filipino homes.

To provide variety, I also performed puppet shows with Bible characters. The favorite shows were Three Men in the Fiery Furnace and Daniel in the Lion's Den. When the lion appeared to growl at Daniel, I raised my voice to its loudest shout and children screamed with fright and delight.

We followed the chalk drawing or puppet show with a gospel message by a Filipino evangelist from the school. To keep attention focused, we used a series of filmstrips depicting the life of Christ.

Two months of meetings provided the listeners with a knowledge of Jesus' life and ministry. The purpose of the tent evangelism was to win souls for Christ. The long-range goal was to plant a local church so the fruit would remain.

Recognizing the importance of preserving the fruit of the evangelism, we followed up the prospects through visitation and Bible study. We instructed the new Christians in the significance and meaning of baptism and church membership.

During the meetings, we looked for a location where we could construct a simple chapel of bamboo and palm leaves. When the campaign came to a close, we arranged a baptismal service for those who had confessed Christ as Savior. We typically baptized 25 new believers and organized them into a local church with the visiting student graduate in charge, subsidized by funds from ABWE.

We could only do tent evangelism when it was not typhoon season. During the typhoon-prone months of May through October, I went to several struggling mission stations and held evangelistic campaigns in the churches

Bill Hopper plays the accordion.

to encourage their growth. I purposely did not keep a tally of the churches I planted. Let God get the glory. But the efforts of my team must have resulted in at least ten churches planted, and a score more of small missions strengthened through these evangelism efforts.

Stationed in Bacolod, I did surveys, learning which towns had no evangelistic witness. I then would go and conduct evangelistic meetings in one of those villages for a month. By that time, we usually had enough new believers to start a new church. I then placed the Bible student there as pastor of the flock. It was an effective method before the days of electronic media.

The campaign in San Carlos

I remember the tent evangelism campaign in San Carlos in Negros Occidental for several reasons. We providentially gained favor with the mayor who issued us a permit to set up our tent in this staunch Catholic sugar milling town.

After setting up the tent, we installed an amplifier in the Jeep and strapped the loudspeaker to the luggage rack and drove through the town playing music, announcing the evangelistic meetings, and tossing tracts out the window as we went.

We stopped in one narrow street, tossed out some tracts, and children came running from every direction to pick them up. When we started to go again, something seemed to be hindering the Jeep. I thought the back wheels might have stopped in one of the many potholes and was ready to gun the motor when people shouted at me, "Stop! A child is under the Jeep!"

I got out and ran to the rear just as the people dragged a small boy from under the vehicle. There were tire marks on his shirt, but he didn't seem to be injured. As a precaution, I sent the child and mother to the hospital, and X-rays confirmed that the boy was not injured, just scared to death.

The meetings got underway, and the people turned out. A couple with two small children attended the tent meeting every night and showed interest in the gospel messages. They responded to an invitation for salvation and attended the Bible studies after the meetings. When we talked to them about baptism and church membership, they told us, "We are not married." We arranged for them to marry in a simple ceremony and they were among the first members of the new church.

Their living was provided by buying and selling fish. They would go to the seashore before dawn to buy a supply of fish from the fishermen who had been out all night.

They would sell the fish for a small profit in a market stall during the day.

Being taught about family devotions, they started having their praise and prayers before going to buy the day's supply of fish. They lived in a very crowded area where houses were wall to wall. Their singing at 3 or 4 a.m. disturbed their neighbors. Their solution to the complaints, they told us, was to pinch the baby so it would cry, and then they could sing for the crying baby (an acceptable Filipino custom).

Another unforgettable character in San Carlos was Mr. Batongmalaki (meaning "hard stone"). He was the neighborhood drunkard and abuser. When he was drunk, he became very wild. He had been known to pull down a bamboo and palm leaf house when someone agitated him.

When he was already too drunk to keep going, he would stagger into the tent and plop himself down on one of the benches. He always found a place to sit, even on a crowded bench, because people were afraid of him and always moved over to make room.

Night after night he continued to come and sprawl and sleep on the bench. The Word of God penetrated his drunken stupor. He began to sober up and listen. He made a profession of faith, was baptized, and became a member of the Fundamental Baptist Church of San Carlos.

Fellowship Baptist Church, San Carlos

The change in his life was very evident to his neighbors. No more drunken rampages disturbed the tranquility of the neighborhood. But Batongmalaki then became self-righteous and a bit of a Pharisee. One time, when he decided the people of the congregation were not conducting church to suit him, he placed a padlock on the door of the little bamboo and nipa (palm leaves) chapel. It took a meeting with him and some frank counseling to get the church open for worship again.

Today, San Carlos has become a city. The church has grown through the years, and a permanent building provides a place to worship.

CHAPTER 6

The Trip to Hinubaan

"**C**ome and help us." The call came from Hinubaan, one of the most remote barrios (villages) in Negros Occidental. From May to October, the threat of typhoons made it dangerous to pursue our usual tent campaigns, so we used the opportunity to augment the evangelistic ministry of smaller churches.

This call offered an opportunity to visit and help a church we had not reached before. There was no road going to Hinubaan. Only small bancas (outrigger canoes) provided daily transportation for the one-thousand residents. The only way to get there from Bacolod City was to take a banca or drive to the end of the road and then hike over the mountains.

But a banca could not accommodate Dorothy and me, Barbara 12, Dee 8 and David 5 plus a Philippine evangelist. So, we took a ferry boat to Iloilo, found a batile (small sailing vessel) hauling lumber to Hinubaan, and boarded the boat that evening. There were no staterooms; we all laid our pallets on deck to spend the night.

The voyage relied on wind power alone and would take 14 hours. But the seas were calm and the wind favorable. We all slept soundly as we were rocked gently in the cradle of the deep.

At dawn, I was awakened by a commotion and shouts for help. I ran toward the stern and found our Filipino evangelist hanging over the side of the boat. He had risen early to relieve himself in the boat's toilet, which consisted of a wooden box with a hole in the floor wired to the outside of the railing. The pastor had climbed into the box, but some of the rusted wires had broken, and was dangling with pastor hanging on—and his pants also were falling off. The sailor who had been controlling the tiller joined me as we rescued our companion from a dunking in the sea. We laughed much later together about this incident.

When we arrived at the shore the next morning, men from the village waded out to carry us and the cargo to

This batile carried the Hoppers to Hinubaan.

shore. We were greeted by a curious crowd of residents. They had never seen a white woman or white children. Their contact with Americans had been limited to a few GIs during WW ll.

The church members had renovated a house for us, complete with the first toilet in Hinubaan, consisting of a cubbyhole with a hole in the floor with a large pit beneath it.

Our children basked in their popularity as the three white-skinned blondes always found themselves surrounded by the brown-skinned, black-headed children. They all delighted in playing along the seashore just a few yards from our house. The local children would call to us saying, "David is taking a bath again" (probably the fourth or fifth time). Filipinos usually go swimming (called a bath) only once a day.

In the meetings, our evangelist preached with the Life of Christ filmstrips (no movies in those days) and I shared the gospel while drawing blacklight chalk drawings. There was no electricity in the village, and nearly the whole barrio turned out to see the lights and special effects our generator allowed.

People who had never before heard the gospel were enlightened and the congregation was encouraged.

Onward to Sipalay

After we finished the meetings in Hinubaan, we hiked north several miles to Tabuan, a smaller barrio of Sipalay town. The believers there had asked us to have meetings in their small chapel before returning to Bacolod.

Our accommodations were with a dear elderly widow. She moved the rest of her family out to make room for us. In the sala (living room) of her small house, she had placed a beautiful bronze casket. It was the one provided by the government for her son who had been killed fighting the rebels. When she buried his body, she was afraid thieves would dig up the casket to steal it. So, she placed the body in a local wooden box and set the casket on its stand in the middle of the living room. For want of space, she put a mat for David under the casket. Of course, he was not happy about that, and we took him onto our grass mat bed.

One afternoon we heard David shouting for help. Following the sound, we found him out in the wide yard being chased by a big tom turkey. He was losing the race, and the turkey knocked him down and spanked him with his wings before we were able to rescue the frightened little boy.

During the week a storm, the edge of a typhoon, came sweeping in over the island. As a result, the sea was very rough, and we were forced to delay our trip home. When, after a week, the storm abated, we decided to take an outrigger along the coast in an attempt to reach the end of the

The outrigger boat took the Hoppers the first leg of their journey back to home base.

road in Inayawan. The men loaded us and our cargo on the boat. It was overloaded, but they were confident that they could sail with it.

Bouncing and diving through the waves, we sailed until we arrived at a sheltered bay. There we were told we had to leave the boat and walk the rest of the way. They said the sea ahead of us was so turbulent and tricky to navigate that sailors were afraid to take passengers through it.

The end of the road was still several miles away over the rolling hills. Off we trudged, Evangelist Catanus, Dorothy, Barbara, Dee, David and I in a little line. We followed the well-traveled trail up and down in the tropical heat of the day. The mood was kept happy by our jolly pastor as he talked to the little kids and encouraged them to keep going. Finally, David gave up as his little legs could carry him no further. The Filipino picked him up and carried him "piggyback" the rest of the way.

The pastor of the church in Inawayan graciously made room for us, since we had to wait until early morning for the bus. I was assigned to a cot. As soon as I lay down, I discovered it was wet with the baby's urine that quickly soaked through my blanket. Never mind. When you are that tired, any place of rest will do.

After the night of rest, we crossed the river on a raft and boarded the truck that had been fitted with wooden benches to carry passengers the five-hour trip on the dusty, unpaved roads to Bacolod City.

When we arrived at the bus terminal, I planned to take a public Jeepney to our house. Dorothy said, "No way, we look like a bunch of refugees. Take a taxi so people won't stare at us."

We were two weeks late returning. When we arrived home, the house girls greeted us with hugs and tears. They had been afraid that we had been lost in the storm. We were all happy to be "home" again.

We held our last campaign in Negros Occidental in 1957.

CHAPTER 7

A Time of Transition

In 1959 we went to Negros Oriental. The Presbyterians had quit preaching the true gospel, and ABWE felt they were therefore not only free to invade the Presbyterian territory, but felt the Lord was challenging them to take the gospel there. In doing so, we got more opposition from the Presbyterians than we got from the Catholics.

We began a campaign and started a church in Dumaguete, the capital of Negros Oriental. We purchased land and built a house for ourselves and a student center for students of Silliman University, started by Dr. Hubbard.

By the time we got there, the school and churches in the area had gone thoroughly modernistic. There was a need to bring the gospel to the students and population.

The American head of the divinity program at Silliman wrote a letter to all the churches warning them against the Baptists invading the territory because they were teaching—and he listed all their Baptist distinctives—"none of which we believe."

That publicity gave the gospel team incentive. Bill wrote a reply saying they were not there to make Presbyterians into Baptists, but to reach any and all who were unsaved. That's why we began the student center, and we called Naomi Hucal to work with Dorothy in the student center. They conducted Bible studies and child evangelism outreaches, and Naomi became very close to us—almost part of the family.

We planted churches there until 1964. Then the mission called me back to be president of the Doane Evangelistic Institute.

At that time Dorothy was diagnosed with breast cancer. Our mission doctor operated on her and felt he had removed all the cancer. After one year the cancer returned throughout her body. In November of 1966, we returned to the States.

When we got to Grand Rapids, the doctor told us she would die within a month. "Just take her home, and we'll give her hospice care and take care of her," he said. That's what we did.

On Christmas morning, Susan prepared breakfast. When I sat down to eat, I remembered I had left the thermometer in Dorothy's mouth. I returned to take it out, and she was gone. She had been in a coma for several weeks. She was 48, the same age as me.

We notified the undertaker, got dressed, and went to church, as it was also Sunday. Susan and I continued to live in Grand Rapids for the next year. We had spent several furloughs in Grand Rapids, and the Berean Baptist Church there had provided us a house to live in. The church then called me to be its visitation pastor.

Susan, our youngest, was 9 years old. David was finishing high school, Diane was in nurse's training, and Barbara was already married.

A new wife and mother

It was quite evident that Susan needed a mother. The Lord laid it on my heart to court Naomi, back in Negros.

Naomi was a graduate of Doane and had been a full-time Christian worker for 12 years, but had never married. When we went to Negros Oriental, the mission invited her to join the team. There were two women ministers of visitation, one graduate evangelist, and I.

I wrote to Naomi's father requesting his permission to

ask Naomi to marry me. Her father responded from the book of Ruth, "Let your people be her people, and your God her God." Naomi welcomed the invitation, and we planned a wedding for July 11, 1967 in Hawaii.

When I informed ABWE that I was intending to marry Naomi, I got a surprise reaction. "You can't do that; you can't marry a native," they said.

"I'm not asking your permission," I responded. "I'm letting you know what I am planning on doing."

"If you marry her, you can't come back to the Philippines." Though there was no rule in ABWE's policies against marrying a native, the mindset of the 1940s lingered on.

"It is inevitable that missionary men are going to marry on the field," I told them, "and you should be prepared for it. What better way to break the ice than with two experienced missionaries?"

So we went forward with the marriage, holding no grudge against the ABWE leadership for espousing what was entrenched practices in the mission world at that time, yet believing there would come a time when all of us would look at things in a better light.

I thought we could get married in Hawaii—kind of a half-way point for both of us. But the U.S. embassy would not give her a fiancé visa to allow Naomi to leave the country. So I flew to Manila, and we were married there.

I was 49 and Naomi was 37. There was a 15-day waiting period after getting a marriage license. I immediately went to the U.S. embassy to get a visa for Naomi to come to the U.S.

"She has to have an interview," the official said, "and I don't have an opening right now. But as soon as you're officially married, come back and see me."

The day after the marriage, I went to see him. "Have you been praying?" he asked.

Bill and Naomi on their wedding day

"Yes."

He sent us down the hall to an American woman who did the interviewing. She was a tough, hatchet-faced type of person. I expected she would turn me down.

"What makes you think you can get an interview?" she asked.

"I've been praying."

"Well," she said, "I just happen to have a cancellation for tomorrow morning at 8 o'clock."

"Praise the Lord!"

We stayed in a hotel across the street from the embassy and were at the embassy the next morning at 7. The place was packed with people. We sat down and waited patiently until 8 o'clock. Then I went to the window and said, "I was supposed to have an appointment at 8 o'clock, and I have not been called."

"Who gave you this appointment?"

I told her.

"I'll call her."

The lady thought my papers were probably stuck in one of the stacks of documents of the Filipino secretaries that did the paperwork. She searched through the piles of papers, found our application, shoved it at one of the Filipino secretaries and said, "Do this one! Now!"

She interviewed Naomi.

Bill said, "This is Tuesday, and I have reservations to fly on Thursday."

"No way!"

"I've been praying."

Naomi and I got the visa and flew back to Grand Rapids on our scheduled flight.

Susan was so happy. It was like a mother coming home to her child, and the older children had no problem with it, either.

I resumed my services as visitation pastor for Berean Baptist Church in Grand Rapids.

Grand Rapids then was a racially prejudiced town. Friends I had known for years now would have nothing to do with us. At the same time, many others embraced and appreciated us both. It also was a test of Naomi's spirituality, as she totally ignored the prejudicial attitudes and actions. She remained her sweet, gentle self.

Our first priority was to ask, "Lord, what would you have us do?"

During that time there was a group of Christians who started a financial planning company. The devil whispered in my ear, "You've worked long enough as a missionary; stay here and do well for yourself." These Christians felt I had the mindset and abilities to do well in the business, but I had no inclination to accept a position with them. I continued to turn them down for the next six months.

I candidated at a church, but neither of us felt that it was God's direction.

Then one day I received a letter from Frank Hooper, a classmate of mine at Moody. Frank was then a missionary in Puerto Rico under the auspices of United Faith Mission. He operated a Christian service men's center and church for the military serving in Roosevelt Road's Naval Station. It was the largest naval air station that the U.S. had at that time. Hundreds of families were stationed there, as well as a large contingent of Seabees. He had property and buildings right outside the base gate, and his church was the only English-speaking church in the area.

In his prayer letter he wrote, "Pray with us as we need another couple to work with us."

I contacted him, and Frank replied, "Come down and see if this is what the Lord wants you to do."

To work with him, we would have to join another mission.

CHAPTER 8

Puerto Rico — Hawaii

O ur daughter Ruth was born in June of 1968. Ruth was only six weeks old when we left for Puerto Rico, and ten-year-old Susan joyously tagged along. Dee Ann remained behind to complete her nurse's training, David had graduated from high school and was working for a Christian electrical contractor, and Barbara was married.

We took charge of the Christian Servicemen's Center in Ceiba. I held Bible studies and witnessed, and Naomi prepared meals for the young men who showed up—anywhere from two to twenty men. Because we did not find an English-speaking school for Susan to attend, she went to a boarding school in Takoa Falls, Georgia. After one year, a Christian navy couple took her to New York State and enrolled her in Appalachian Christian School.

After two years I was asked to pastor the English-speaking Grace Bible Church connected with the Servicemen's Center. Attendance ranged from 150 to 200 per Sunday. We have kept in touch with several of the church members over the years. Our son Billy was born in June 1969. He has a Puerto Rican Spanish birth certificate.

After four years (two years in the servicemen's center and two years in the church), we were due for furlough. One of the United Faith Mission board members con-

The church Bill pastored in Puerto Rico was also a servicemen's center.

tacted me and asked if we would be interested in taking an assignment in Hawaii. We had made inquiries about going to Hawaii before accepting the appointment to Puerto Rico, but nothing then had opened up.

The United Faith Mission had a mission in Hawaii that was not producing. Over a period of twelve years,

Under Bill's leadership the Hawaiian mission outgrew its facility and sold it to the Korean Baptists.

they had sent nine men there, but none of them had stayed much more than a year. The challenge was to go there, take over the mission, and either cure it or bury it.

We accepted the challenge and arrived in 1972. My years of experience proved the difference in the outcome. I learned after I arrived that the other young pastors had been dominated by a local man in the church, who—

because he was older than they—thought he knew best how to run things. Also, the young men had difficulty adapting to life on the relatively confined island. This time, I was older than the local man, and he respected me. Naomi and I already had 20 or more years working as missionaries on an island, so we had no difficulty adjusting to the circumstances in Hawaii. As an American-Asian couple, we fit well into the culture.

We were located in Palolo Valley, part of Honolulu, about 15 miles from the naval station. We conducted worship and services for families and children in the valley where the church was located. I made some contacts with the Navy and developed a servicemen's center at the church. I preached to the families, and we offered hospitality to the servicemen and the families that attended church. We would later learn the fruit of our ministry. From those servicemen, five became pastors, and two became foreign missionaries. Some of them are still supporting our ministry. (Bill's preaching and Naomi's cinnamon rolls made an impact!)

We expanded the worship area on the covered patio to accommodate the increasing number of worshipers. We often invited churchgoers into our home for a meal.

We were supposed to get $1000/mo., but I had been able to raise only $700 per month support. New families were added, and after three years we decided to formally organize the church in 1975. The church was self-supporting and decided to go independent. They installed me as the pastor of the church and offered to pay me $500 per month.

We remained in the house church for 13 years, while continuing our ministry to the servicemen. The church grew, children grew up, and young couples married in the church—and Naomi made all the wedding cakes. The patio would hold only 100, and as attendance increased, we had to go to two services. This led us to pray for a better location.

In 1980 one of the members told me about a large piece of land just up the street that was for sale. The owners were an elderly couple in process of getting a divorce.

The mission dedicated a newly constructed church
building on new property in 1985.

Land in Hawaii is sold by the square foot, and they were asking $640,000 for 53,000 sq. ft. with six rental houses on it. I bargained them down to $480,000. We didn't have the cash, so they leased the land to us with an option to buy. The rentals from the houses made the mortgage payments, which were applied to the principal.

After five years we approached the bank for a loan to cover the balance of the price and start a new building. Since we still had the big house for equity, the bank loaned us $650,000—enough to pay the rest of the purchase price and build the new church. After the new church was constructed, we sold the old property to a Korean Baptist Church for $450,000, allowing us to pay off the loan ahead of schedule.

I met this real estate attorney, Melvin Kaneshige, a Harvard graduate. I led him to Christ, and he became a member of the church.

The large lot went up the side of a mountain, with the back two-thirds undeveloped, like a jungle. The houses were down by the street. We had to decide: should we put the church at the street level, or should we put it at the base of the mountain? We decided to place the church near the street. But code required that if we did that, we would have to destroy the six houses. I insisted we not destroy those houses. It took Melvin a year, but he was finally able to get the land rezoned to a small housing project, enabling them to leave the six houses there.

We put the church in front and a parking lot behind it. We developed the back section into three levels or tiers, with retaining walls sustaining each in front. We moved three of the houses to the rear-most and highest level, two on the intermediate level, and one plus a new parsonage on the first level. The site work alone cost us more than the church building.

I remained pastor for 17 years. When I turned 70 in 1988, I told the church they should get a younger pastor. I had seen older men ruin a church by staying too long. It took them almost a year, and they called Robert Field from Canada to be the new pastor. I officially resigned in 1989.

When Pastor Field came to the church, Naomi and I went to the Philippines and Thailand to visit fellow workers we had known 27 years earlier.

Robert Field pastored the church from 1989 to 2008, when he decided to go back to Canada to take care of his elderly mother. He recommended that the church call Billy, our youngest son, to pastor the church.

Billy was then principal of Hanalani Schools, a Christian school in Mililani, Hawaii. He had been there for 16 years, first as a teacher, and then as principal. When they extended the call to him, he called us, then in Thailand, to ask our opinion. Through my tears of

Today, Hopper's son, Billy, pastors the
Honolulu Bible Church.

joy, I said, "Go for it." I didn't tell him I had been praying for that for years.

During our visit to the Philippines, I spoke at the
anniversary of Doane Baptist Seminary (as the Doane
Evangelistic Institute had become) and then went on
to visit Filipino missionaries in Thailand. The Filipino
Baptist missionaries had formed PABWE, the Philippine
Association of Baptists for World Evangelism in 1957,
and Thailand was the first country where they went. The
students we had once taught were now the missionaries
running things.

The Filipinos had started an English-speaking church
in Thailand. They asked us to take over that church for a
year. We went there in 1990 and pastored for two years.

That was where we met Pete and Melody Wong, then working in Thailand under PABWE from 1986 to 1996, and now working with Advancing Native Missions since 2013.

CHAPTER 9

Leyte Baptist Seminary

After two years of pastoring the English-speaking church for missionaries and English-speaking foreigners in Thailand, we came back to Hawaii in 1992.

We lived in one of the rental units of our former church that the church had assigned to me for life.

We visited the Philippines every year. When we visited the Philippines in 1989, Pastor Malanday, pastor of the church in Maasin on Leyte Island, told me he wanted to start a Bible school. Did I have any books I would be willing to donate? I packed up my entire library and sent it

The librarian sorts some of the books Bill Hopper
donated from his personal library.

to Maasin. This new-founded school named their library
Hopper Library.

In 1992 while in Hawaii, I received a letter from Pastor
Malanday asking if I would come and help with the Bible
school. We prayed about it and contacted ABWE. I told
them that we had been invited to go to the Philippines
to start a Bible school. What was their attitude about our
going back?

They answered, "That is no problem at all."

With that endorsement, I wrote Pastor Malanday and
said: "I need more authority in the invitation. I can't come
just because you alone invited me."

A little while later, I received a letter signed by all the
pastors of the East Visayan Fellowship of Fundamental

Baptist Churches asking me to come as director of the Bible school.

We accepted the call and returned to the Philippines in 1993 to serve as the director of the Bible school in Maasin. The school was meeting in the building of the Baptist Church of Maasin.

The church also hosted a Christian academy. We were trying to teach theology in one corner of the worship hall, and someone was conducting a second-grade class in another corner of the worship hall. It was bedlam.

The students were housed in temporary sheds that had been added to the church—not fit for human residence. They were terrible.

I told the school board, "The school will never advance until you have your own campus."

My closest assistant was David Epilepcia. He was pastoring a church in Macrohon, about 10 km. outside Maasin, and teaching in the school. That first year I encouraged him to become the president of the school. I was convinced that Filipino schools should be under the authority of Filipino leaders. We also changed the name to Leyte Baptist Seminary, as Filipinos recognized a seminary as a theological school for the training of ministers.

After one year, I told David: I'm going to go through the States to raise funds to obtain a campus for this school. I

Bill Hopper sold his Toyota SUV to help buy
land for the seminary.

sold my SUV for $3,000 and left the money with Pastor
Epilepcia as seed money to help buy land.

Filipino Nelson Tan was helping us look for land.
He was the head of the highway department on Leyte
Island. While we were in the States, Engineer Tan wrote
me that he had found five acres of land for sale 5 km.
outside of Maasin. It was an abandoned coconut grove,
and the price was 7 pesos per sq. meter or $5,000 total. I
wrote him back: take the money from the car and secure
the land.

Meanwhile, in 1994 we visited 51 churches in the
U.S. presenting the challenge of the Bible school in the
Philippines. They welcomed us and gave us an offering,

with many promises of support. After nine months, we had acquired $40,000, even though only one church put us on their regular budget—Bethel Bible Church in Hawaii where we worshiped.

We named the campaign the Philippine Evangelism Training Project (PET). We needed someone to handle donations in the U.S., as pastor Bob Field did not want to do it. We met the president of ABWE and asked him if we could channel our donations through ABWE. "Absolutely," he responded. ABWE made PET an official project and regarded us as official volunteers. So, everyone who sent their donations to ABWE got a tax-deductible receipt.

John Lindner met the Hoppers when he
visited Leyte in 1995.

In 1995 I returned to Philippines. The school now had $40,000 and 5 acres of land. I consulted with Engineer Tan. He was willing to help us build some buildings. I suggested putting up temporary bamboo and palm leaf structures until we got money to construct permanent buildings.

"I wouldn't do that," he immediately replied. "The first typhoon that comes through here, all your buildings will be destroyed. Let's take the $40,000 and build the first building as a permanent, concrete block building. It won't be eaten by the termites nor destroyed by the storms."

So that's what we did. The first building accommodated three classrooms and a library. Leyte Baptist Seminary was on the map.

First of all, we had to clear the lot of old, dead coconut trees. The Philippine Highway Department of Leyte helped clear the land without charge; we just paid for the fuel.

While we were in the process of building one of the faculty cottages, we ran out of money. I told the workers, "If we don't have $3,000 by next week, we'll have to stop construction and wait for the money. So, everybody, please pray that the money will come in."

On Monday we received information from ABWE that $3,000 had just come in. It was a gift from a Japanese neurosurgeon in Japan, whom I had led to the Lord while he was working in Honolulu. He then returned to Japan and became head of a big hospital there. His gift arrived with perfect timing.

Engineer Tan did all of the engineering and signing for no salary. As we finished one building, the Lord brought in more money, and step by step we built an academic building, a library, six three-bedroom cottages for our faculty members, a men's dorm, women's dorm, caretaker's cottage, a kindergarten, and a canteen. Naomi and I built our own house with our own money on the campus. LBS then had 14 buildings on its campus, each beautifully designed, and laid out in a pleasant pattern.

We organized the school and were approved as a legitimate organization by the Philippine Department of Education. The school soon had 80 students. We elected David Epelipcia president of the school, while I continued to conduct a full schedule of teaching. We occupied the whole campus in 1995 with four faculty members. Writer John Lindner also visited us at that time.

We wanted to have a church associated with the seminary. A pastor who owned a neighboring lot donated a portion of it for the church, which we called Leyte Baptist Seminary Mission. Today it is doing well, with a pastor who is a graduate of LBS. People attend from four or five nearby communities. Faculty attend the church on campus when they are not out speaking in other churches.

We had funds for the PET project, funds for the school, and then we added financing for subsidizing pastors and church planting. We did this in cooperation with New Life Mission, a local Filipino mission with 25 outreaches sponsored by the New Life Baptist Church in Tacloban, the provincial capital. To have financial accountability for our church-planting subsidies, we channel the funds through that mission.

Following the example of the apostle Paul, we visit the school and church plants every year. We keep in contact by email and continue to raise funds for subsidies.

In 2004 we felt led to stay in Hawaii and not go back to teach in the school, which was God's providence. In November I had triple bypass surgery.

After David Epilepcia, LBS had several presidents. During our visit in 2016 the current president, Pastor Mabanag, discovered he had a brain tumor and resigned. But there was no one to take over the school. We stayed on as the interim school president for the 2016-2017 school year. We conducted a search for a new president, and finally installed Bert Nasayao, an experienced administrator and educator from Tacloban.

We went again this year for six weeks, March 12 to April 30, 2019. We attended the commencement of the seminary, and was invited to be the baccalaureate speaker. During Holy Week each year, we have the annual conference of all the Baptist churches in East Visayas (Leyte and Samar), attended by 800 to 1,000 people. We connected with all the pastors without traveling throughout the provinces to visit them all.

Naomi and I continue to raise funds for the PET project, which supports the seminary, church planting projects, and outreach among the Ati.

TO BE CONTINUED . . .

EPILOGUE
The Ati March Forward

Rogelio "Roger" Elosendo was from the Ati tribe, the aborigines of the Philippines. Diminutive in stature, dark-skinned, and curly-haired, these nomads lived in the mountains of Northern Luzon and Panay Islands. They are disadvantaged economically, educationally and socially; most are illiterate.

Rogelio's Uncle Severo was head of an Ati village in Iloilo when American missionary William Hopper vowed to evangelize them. When lowlanders heard of his intentions, many responded, *Why bother? Those people don't even have souls.* But Hopper was insistent.

At the same time, the Atis had heard that the Americans would capture them and use them as fuel in the sugar mill. But Severo wanted to learn the truth. He became Hopper's first convert and disciple and subsequently led many other Atis to Christ, including his nephew, Rogelio (pron. Rohelio). Rogelio promised his uncle that he would become a missionary to his own people. Severo became known as Tata Vero (Father Vero) by the whole Ati community.

Rogelio enrolled at Doane as Severo had done years earlier and did janitorial work to pay his expenses. When he graduated in 1988, the church in Padada called him.

Not long after he arrived, Rogelio stood up during a congregational meeting and announced that he had one last item for the agenda. "I want to marry the Bible woman," he said. "I have one problem, though," he told the elders; "The Bible woman doesn't like me."

Stunned by Rogelio's declaration, Sylvia, herself a lowlander, said in her heart, "Yes, Lord, I do want to marry a pastor so we can be partners in the ministry. But, Lord, an Ati?" Evidently, Rogelio was not what Sylvia had in mind. He wore ill-fitting shoes and clothes, and his hair was unkempt.

The elders assured Rogelio they would court Sylvia for him. They told Sylvia, "Rogelio is good in music. He's intelligent, a good preacher, and a godly man."

They even bought him new clothes and a new pair of shoes. After much thought and prayer, Sylvia agreed to marry the Ati pastor.

A new ministry together

Rogelio did not forget his promise to Tatay Vero. He and his young wife left Davao del Sur in 1990 and returned to Panay Island and his uncle's church. Tatay Vero was so happy to see him back—it was an answer to his prayers! In fact, Tatay Vero appointed him as his successor to carry on the ministry before he left this earth in 2004.

Rogelio and Sylvia only had a few pesos when they arrived, and life did not get easier. The Sunday offering of the Ati church was almost nothing, and the work was replete with trials and challenges both unfamiliar and daunting. They subsisted on Ati food such as snails, frogs, snakes, lizards, and cassava. Sylvia had never eaten such food, but she determined she would learn to live the Ati way or starve. Through these trials, God taught her to be a humble and effective servant.

In 1993 Rogelio and Sylvia founded Ati Tribes Mission to point the Ati people to Christ. They dreamed of lifting Rogelio's people out of their miserable state and showing them a better life. Sylvia's heart ached especially for the Ati children, who could not obtain medical care when they got sick simply because they were Atis. That led them to begin a children's home the next year.

Rogelio and Sylvia wanted to establish an Ati community where they could teach the Ati proper hygiene and social responsibility, as well as simple livelihood projects, such as gardening and handicraft. Above all, they would engage them in Bible study and worship services.

One day in 2010 as Rogelio was walking through an area of Iloilo, he saw an old, disheveled Ati woman sprawled on a dirty sidewalk. Rogelio stopped and tried to wake her up. When he saw her face, he burst into tears: It was a distant cousin!

"Manang" (older sister), he whispered, "Bo Barredo has asked me to come to America soon, and I will ask God's people to help us establish a decent community for all of us."

A dream coming true

Rogelio and Sylvia had met Bo Barredo, then President of Advancing Native Missions, in 1990, and through the resulting partnership their dream began to be realized. It all came to a head on February 3, 2017.

Through ANM, American believers helped the Elosendos purchase an acre of land near Iloilo City. Rogelio, like Uncle Vero before him, became a friend to the mayor of Iloilo, and he, in turn, used community funds to pave the road from the Ati community to the public school so the Ati children could get an education without walking through the mud. Another NGO provided low-cost housing for many Ati families. And with funds generated through ANM, a new church was constructed. The worship hall is on the second floor while the ground floor houses an Ati children's center. All were dedicated to the Lord on that day.

In February, 2017 the Ati dedicated a new church constructed with the help of Advancing Native Missions.

In addition, more than 50 Ati believers were baptized in a baptismal tank constructed for the occasion, more than a dozen Ati mothers brought their babies forward for dedication, and a dozen Ati couples who had been living together common-law sealed their commitment with a mass Christian wedding ceremony.

Rogelio and Sylvia have trained several Ati pastors, and the ministry now has eight churches under his oversight in the 21 areas targeted for Ati outreach in Antique Province. Altogether there are some 80 Ati churches on Panay and Guimaras Islands.

Rogelio and Sylvia give God all the glory. As Sylvia puts it, "Each day is a brand-new opportunity for us to allow God to continue His creative work."

And to think it all started with the conversion of one Ati chief through the determined efforts of one American missionary—William Hopper. To God be the glory.

About the Author

John Lindner has devoted the last 40 years of his life to missionary journalism. He is the author of two books and the editor of several others. He was awarded a Doctor of Mission Degree by the Evangelical Theological Seminary in Kota, Rajasthan in recognition of his lifetime achievement. He was recently designated a lifetime member of the Evangelical Press Association.

The Ministry
of ANM

**ANM Publications is a ministry initiative
of Advancing Native Missions**

Advancing Native Missions (ANM) is a U.S.-based Christian missions agency. However, unlike many such agencies that are involved in sending missionaries from America to other places around the world, ANM works with indigenous missionaries. Indigenous (or native) missionaries are Christian workers who minister within their own sphere of influence proclaiming the Gospel of Jesus Christ to their own people. ANM then works to connect Christians in America with these brothers and sisters, to equip and encourage them. Our goal is to build relationships of love and trust between indigenous missionaries and

North American individuals and churches. In this way, the entire body of Christ becomes involved in completing the Great Commission. *"And this gospel of the kingdom shall be preached in all the world as a witness to all nations, and then the end shall come"* (Matthew 24:14).

If you would like to know how you can become an effective coworker with native missionaries to reach the unreached for Jesus Christ, contact ANM at contact@ AdvancingNativeMissions.com, call us at 540-456-7111, or visit our website: www.AdvancingNative Missions.com.

CPSIA information can be obtained
at www.ICGtesting.com
Printed in the USA
LVHW090139301121
704796LV00002B/62